12 snacks

36 sides

58 curries

80 big dishes

108 extras

124 desserts

140 index

C is for Caribbean contains 50 of the most definitive

and delicious recipes in modern Caribbean cooking.

C is for Caribbean ingredients

ackee is a scarlet pear-shaped fruit related to the lychee. It is the national fruit of Jamaica where it is widely eaten. It is available canned.

breadfruit is a starchy fruit used in both savoury and sweet dishes.

calabaza pumpkin is a large winter squash grown throughout the Caribbean. It has a sweet taste and can be used in both savoury and sweet dishes. If you can't find it use butternut squash instead.

callaloo is one of the main staple leafy greens in Caribbean cooking. It has a slightly bitter flavour and resembles spinach. It is mostly steamed and eaten as a side dish.

goat is eaten in stews and curries. It tastes similar to lamb but is leaner. If you can't find goat then use lamb instead.

jerk seasoning is a medium-hot blend of spices, which is used to rub on pork or chicken before cooking.

okra (also called ladies fingers because of its long cylindical shape) is a nutritious green vegetable eaten in salads, curries or as a side dish.

pigeon peas are widely used in Caribbean cooking. If you can't find them use kidney beans or black-eyed beans instead.

plantain belongs to the banana family. It is inedible raw so must be cooked first. Fried plantain is a popular snack or side dish in the Caribbean.

salted cod is dried cod that has been salted. It needs to be rehydrated and de-salted before use by soaking in a bowl of water for at least 4 hours and changing the water every hour.

scotch bonnet chillies are small but extremely hot. They are used throughout the Caribbean and have a sweet fruity flavour. They are one of the main ingredients in West Indian hot pepper sauces.

sweet potato is a large starchy root vegetable with pink-orange skin and deep orange flesh. It has a sweet, creamy flavour and can be used in a variety of dishes.

turmeric is a bright yellow spice with lots of health benefits and is a major ingredient in curries. Use carefully as it stains.

(Some Caribbean ingredients are available from large supermarkets or specialist grocery shops. However, it is also worth checking online through suppliers such as gracefoods.co.uk or olumofoods.co.uk or sams247.com)

(snacks)

saltfish fritters

makes ●●●
　　　　 ●●●

prep

soak

cook

---

ingredients

250g (9oz) salted cod
½ red (bell) pepper,
　finely chopped
½ onion, finely chopped
½ Scotch bonnet chilli,
　finely chopped
1 egg
200g (7oz/1½ cups) plain
　(all-purpose) flour
sea salt and freshly ground
　black pepper

1 litre (34fl oz/4 cups)
　vegetable oil, to deep-fry

soak

Place the salted cod in a bowl of cold water and soak for 4 hours, changing the water every hour.

mix

Flake the salted cod finely with a fork or in a food processor, then mix with the red pepper, onion, chilli, egg, black pepper and 150ml (5fl oz/⅔ cup) water. Stir in the flour to form a wet batter.

fry

Heat the oil in a wok or saucepan to 180°C (350°F), or until a cube of bread dropped in fizzes and turns golden within 30 seconds. Carefully drop heaped tablespoons of batter into the hot oil (you will get about 5 in one pan) and fry for 2 minutes on each side until golden brown and crisp. Drain on kitchen paper and repeat until the batter is used up. Serve immediately, sprinkled with sea salt.

doubles

(trinidad & tobago)

serves ●●●●

makes ●●●●● ●●●●●

prep

rise/rest **x1**

cook

ingredients

325g (11½oz/scant 2½ cups)
  plain (all-purpose) flour
2 tsp fast-action dried (active
  dry) yeast
½ tsp caster (granulated) sugar
½ tsp ground turmeric
½ tsp freshly ground black
  pepper
½ tsp sea salt

2 Tbsp vegetable oil
1 onion, finely sliced
2 cloves garlic, finely chopped
1 tsp ground cumin
1 tsp Jamaican curry powder
  (see page 112)
1 x 400-g (14-oz) can
  chickpeas, drained and rinsed
1 tsp sea salt

200ml (7fl oz/scant 1 cup)
  vegetable oil, to deep-fry

Jamaican hot pepper sauce,
  to serve

mix

Mix the flour, yeast, sugar, turmeric and pepper
together, then add the salt and 200ml (7fl oz/
scant 1 cup) water. Stir to combine, then knead
briefly into a soft dough. Transfer to an oiled
bowl, cover and leave in a warm place for 1 hour,
or until doubled in size.

stir-fry

Heat the oil in a pan and add the onion and garlic.
Stir-fry on a medium heat for 10 minutes until
golden brown, then add the spices and stir-fry for
a further minute. Add the chickpeas, 300ml (10fl
oz/1¼ cups) water and the salt. Bring to the boil,
then reduce the heat and simmer, uncovered,
for 30 minutes. Taste and add more salt if needed.

divide

Once the dough has doubled in size, punch it
down and divide it into 8 pieces. With lightly oiled
hands, flatten each piece into a circle, or bara,
approximately 10cm (4in) across.

deep-fry

Heat the vegetable oil in a wok or saucepan to
180°C (350°F), or until a cube of bread dropped
in fizzes and turns golden within 30 seconds.
Fry 3 bara at a time for 40 seconds on each side
until golden brown, then drain on kitchen paper.

assemble

Place 2 tablespoons of the chickpeas on half
the bara, add the hot pepper sauce, then top
with another bara before serving.

patties
(jamaica)

ingredients

600g (1lb 5oz/4½ cups) plain (all-purpose) flour
2 scant tsp ground turmeric
300g (10½oz/1¼ cups) cold butter, cubed
1 egg, beaten
sea salt

1 Tbsp vegetable oil
500g (1lb 2oz) minced (ground) beef
1 onion, finely chopped
2 cloves garlic, crushed
1 Scotch bonnet chilli, deseeded and finely chopped
4 sprigs thyme, leaves only
2 tsp Jamaican curry powder (see page 112)
500ml (17fl oz/2 cups) beef stock
3 Tbsp fresh white breadcrumbs

mix

For the pastry, blitz the flour, turmeric, 1 teaspoon salt and butter in a food processor or work together with your hands until it is the texture of fine sand. Add 70ml (2½fl oz/¼ cup) water and pulse or mix until the mixture comes together as a dough. Cover and refrigerate for 20 minutes.

brown

For the filling, heat the vegetable oil in a large frying pan on a medium heat. Add the beef and break up with a spoon, then increase the heat and brown well for 10 minutes, stirring occasionally.

simmer

Add the onion, garlic, chilli, thyme and 1 teaspoon salt and stir-fry for 6–7 minutes until the onion has softened. Add the curry powder and stir-fry for a further minute before adding the stock. Bring to the boil, then reduce the heat and simmer, uncovered, for 25 minutes. Stir through the breadcrumbs, taste and season with salt as needed.

serves ●●●●
●●●
●●●●
●●●

prep ◖

cook **x1**

make

To make the patties, preheat the oven to 200°C (400°F) and line a baking sheet with greaseproof paper. Roll the pastry out on a floured surface until it is 2–3mm (¹⁄₁₆–⅛in) thick, then cut out 8-cm (3¼-in) circles. Place a heaped tablespoon of mixture on one side of each round, brush the edge with egg wash, then fold the pastry over the filling and crimp the edge with a fork. Brush the top with egg wash, then transfer to the baking sheet. Repeat until all the pastry is used up (makes approximately 32).

bake

Bake for 25–30 minutes until golden brown.

04

jerk chicken wings

ingredients

2 Tbsp jerk seasoning
  (see page 115)
2 Tbsp soy sauce
2 spring onions (scallions),
  roughly chopped
2 cloves garlic, peeled
½ white onion, roughly chopped
1 Scotch bonnet chilli, deseeded
2 Tbsp vegetable oil
2 Tbsp dark brown sugar
1 tsp sea salt
800g (1lb 12oz) chicken wings

blitz

Blitz the jerk seasoning, soy sauce, spring onions, garlic, onion, chilli, oil, sugar and salt together in a food processor.

marinate

Rub the marinade all over the chicken wings and refrigerate for 1 hour, or overnight.

roast

Preheat the oven to 170°C (325°F). Transfer the wings to a baking dish and roast for 40 minutes before increasing the oven temperature to 200°C (400°F) and roasting for a further 20 minutes.

rest

Leave the chicken wings to rest for 5 minutes before serving hot.

jerk ribs

serves

prep

marinate over-night

cook x1

ingredients

3 Tbsp jerk seasoning
  (see page 115)
2 tsp sea salt
3 Tbsp dark brown sugar
3 spring onions (scallions),
  roughly chopped
½ white onion, roughly chopped
4 cloves garlic, peeled
5cm (2in) ginger, peeled
2 Scotch bonnet chillies,
  deseeded
2 Tbsp vegetable oil
2 x 500-g (1lb 2-oz) rack of ribs

blitz

Blitz the jerk seasoning, sea salt, sugar, onions, garlic, ginger, chillies and oil together in a food processor.

marinate

Rub the marinade all over the ribs, then cover and refrigerate overnight.

roast

When ready to cook, preheat the oven to 170°C (325°F). Place the ribs in a roasting dish, cover tightly with foil and roast for 1 hour 30 minutes.

barbecue

To finish the ribs, either transfer to a barbecue and cook until well charred on both sides, or remove the foil and increase the heat to 200°C (400°F) for a further 20 minutes until well browned. Slice the cooked ribs and serve immediately.

festival fried dumplings
(jamaica)

ingredients

250g (9oz/generous 1¾ cups)
   plain (all-purpose) flour
100g (3½oz/⅔ cup) coarse
   polenta (cornmeal)
1 tsp baking powder
2 Tbsp caster (granulated) sugar
20g (¾oz/1½ Tbsp) softened
   butter
1 tsp vanilla bean paste or
   extract

1 litre (34fl oz/4 cups) vegetable
   oil, to deep-fry

mix

Mix the flour, polenta, baking powder and sugar
together, then work in the butter until the mixture
resembles fine breadcrumbs. Add 150ml (5fl oz/
⅔ cup) water and vanilla bean paste or extract
and knead briefly until the mixture comes together
as a smooth dough.

rest

Cover the dough and leave to rest at room
temperature for 20 minutes.

deep-fry

Heat the oil to 180°C (350°F), or until a cube of bread
turns golden and fizzes within 30 seconds. Divide
the dough into 16 portions and roll each into a
pointed sausage. Carefully lower each dumpling into
the hot oil and deep-fry 4–5 at a time for about
2 minutes until golden brown. Remove with a slotted
spoon and drain on a plate lined with kitchen paper.
Repeat with the remaining dumplings. Serve hot
with Pepperpot Soup (page 28).

07

pepperpot soup

serves

prep

cook

ingredients

500g (1lb 2oz) floury (mealy)
  potatoes
500g (1lb 2oz) butternut squash
2 Tbsp vegetable oil
1 onion, roughly chopped
1 leek, roughly chopped
2 sticks celery, roughly chopped
2 cloves garlic, minced
4 sprigs thyme
1 Scotch bonnet chilli, deseeded
  and finely chopped
1 tsp sea salt
400ml (14fl oz/1²⁄₃ cups)
  coconut milk
400ml (14fl oz/1²⁄₃ cups)
  vegetable stock
  100g (3½oz) callaloo or
  spinach, chopped
freshly ground black pepper

chop

Peel and cut the potato and butternut squash into
1.5-cm (½-in) dice. Set aside.

cook

Heat the oil in a large saucepan, add the onion,
leek, celery, garlic, thyme, chilli and salt. Mix
well, then cover and soften on a medium heat
for 10–15 minutes, stirring occasionally.

simmer

Add the coconut milk, stock, potato and squash
and simmer, partially covered, for 25 minutes until
the potato and the squash are just cooked through.

season

Add the callaloo or spinach and cook for a further
minute until just wilted. Taste and season with more
sea salt and pepper as needed, then serve hot.

08

fried okra
(jamaica)

serves

prep

cook

ingredients
2 Tbsp vegetable oil
1 onion, finely sliced
2 cloves garlic, minced
½ Scotch bonnet chilli,
   deseeded and finely chopped
175g (6oz) okra, sliced
1 tsp sea salt
freshly ground black pepper

fry
Heat the oil in a large frying pan, add the onion, garlic and chilli and stir-fry on a medium heat for 10 minutes until golden brown.

season
Add the okra and stir-fry for a further 6–7 minutes until softened and cooked through. Season to taste with the sea salt and pepper, and serve hot.

fried okra

hot pepper shrimp

(jamaica)

serves ●●

prep

marinate **x1**

cook

ingredients

200g (7oz) raw tiger prawns
(shrimp), with shells on
3 cloves garlic, minced
1 red Scotch bonnet chilli,
deseeded and finely minced
4–5 sprigs thyme, leaves only
2 tsp sea salt
1 tsp ground allspice
1 tsp freshly ground black
pepper

lime wedges, to serve

marinate

Tip the prawns into a large plastic bag along with
the garlic, chilli, thyme, salt, allspice and black
pepper. Mix well through the bag until the prawns
are evenly coated, then refrigerate for 1 hour.

cook

Bring 50ml (1¾fl oz/scant ¼ cup) water to the
boil in a large saucepan, add the prawns and
reduce the heat to a simmer. Stir constantly for
3–4 minutes until the prawns are pink and lightly
coated in the sauce. Serve immediately with
lime wedges on the side.

(sides)

rice and peas

serves

prep

cook

ingredients

800ml (27fl oz/3⅓ cups) coconut milk

1 x 400-g (14-oz) can kidney beans, rinsed and well drained

2 cloves garlic, peeled and left whole

1 onion, finely chopped

½ tsp ground allspice

1 tsp dried thyme

1 tsp sea salt

400g (14oz/2¼ cups) long-grain rice, rinsed and well drained

boil

Bring the coconut milk, kidney beans, garlic, onion, allspice, thyme and salt to the boil in a large saucepan with a tight-fitting lid.

simmer

Add the rice and stir well. When the coconut milk comes to the boil again, reduce the heat to a very low simmer, then cover and leave for 40 minutes.

steam

After 40 minutes, fluff through the rice, then leave uncovered to steam for 5 minutes.

serve

Serve with any Jamaican curry.

macaroni pie

(creole/trinidad & tobago)

ingredients

400g (14oz/3⅓ cups) macaroni
500ml (17fl oz/generous 2 cups)
  evaporated milk
3 eggs, beaten
200g (7oz/2¼ cups) grated
  strong Cheddar cheese
175g (6oz/1½ cups) grated
  mozzarella cheese
1 tsp sea salt
freshly ground black pepper

cook

Preheat the oven to 200°C (400°F). Bring a large
pan of salted water to the boil, add the macaroni
and cook for 9 minutes. Drain well in a colander.

whisk

Meanwhile, whisk the milk and eggs together in
a bowl, then stir in half the cheese, the salt and
plenty of pepper. Once the pasta is cooked,
stir the cheese mixture through it, then transfer
to a buttered lasagne dish.

bake

Top with the remaining cheese, scatter with more
pepper and bake in the oven for 30 minutes until
the cheese is golden and bubbling. Allow to cool
slightly before cutting into squares and serving.

12

callaloo

serves

prep

cook

ingredients

70g (2½oz) smoked bacon
   lardons
2 cloves garlic, minced
1 onion, finely sliced
½ Scotch bonnet chilli, finely
   chopped
1 sprig thyme
200g (7oz) callaloo or spinach,
   roughly chopped
sea salt and freshly ground
   black pepper

fry

Cook the bacon lardons in a large saucepan on
a low heat for 5 minutes until the fat has rendered
down. Increase the heat and fry for a further
2–3 minutes, stirring frequently, until the bacon
is crisp and golden brown.

stir-fry

Add the garlic, onion, chilli and thyme and stir-fry
for a further 5–6 minutes on a medium heat until
the onion has just softened. Add the callaloo or
spinach and stir fry for 3–4 minutes until completely
wilted. Taste and season as needed with salt and
pepper, and serve hot.

13

plantain wedges

serves

prep

cook

ingredients
2 just-ripe plantains
100ml (3½fl oz/7 Tbsp)
  vegetable oil
sea salt

slice
Peel and slice the plantains into 1-cm (½-in)
diagonal wedges.

fry
Heat the oil in a frying pan and, working in
2 batches, fry the plantain wedges on a medium
heat for 2–3 minutes on each side until golden
brown. Transfer to a plate lined with kitchen
paper, and continue until all the wedges are fried.
Scatter with sea salt and serve with the Fried
Bake (see page 54), Curry Goat (see page 62)
or Chicken Curry (see page 60).

14

stewed pigeon peas

(creole/trinidad & tobago)

serves

prep

cook

ingredients

70g (2½oz) smoked bacon
   lardons
1 onion, finely chopped
1 stick celery, finely chopped
2 cloves garlic, finely chopped
4 sprigs thyme
1 x 400-g (14-oz) can pigeon
   peas or kidney beans,
   drained and rinsed
250ml (8½fl oz/1 cup) chicken
   stock
15g (½oz/¼ cup) fresh parsley,
   finely chopped
sea salt and freshly ground
   black pepper

fry

Cook the bacon lardons in a medium saucepan
on a low heat, stirring frequently, for 4–5 minutes
until the fat has rendered down. Increase the heat
and fry for a further 2 minutes, before adding the
onion, celery, garlic and thyme. Cover with a lid
and soften for 10 minutes, stirring occasionally.

simmer

Add the pigeon peas and stock, and simmer,
covered, for 15 minutes. Stir in the parsley, then
taste and season with salt and pepper as needed.

pelau
(creole/trinidad & tobago)

serves ●●●●○

prep

marinate x1

cook x1

ingredients

300g (10½oz) skinless, boneless
   chicken thighs, diced
4 Tbsp green seasoning
   (see page 110)
2 Tbsp soft brown sugar
1 onion, roughly chopped
1 red (bell) pepper, chopped
1 yellow (bell) pepper, chopped
1 carrot, roughly chopped
1 stick celery, roughly chopped
4 sprigs thyme
200g (7oz/1 cup) easy-cook
long-grain rice
400ml (14fl oz/1⅔ cups)
   coconut milk
1 x 400-g (14-oz) can cooked
   pigeon peas or kidney beans,
   drained and rinsed
2 tsp sea salt

marinate

Mix the chicken thighs with the green seasoning,
then cover and refrigerate for 1 hour, or overnight.

cook

Heat the sugar in a large pan for 3–4 minutes
without stirring, until deep brown and nicely
caramelized. Add the marinated chicken and cook
for 2–3 minutes on each side. Cover and cook for
5–6 minutes before adding the onion, peppers,
carrot, celery and thyme. Stir briefly, then cover and
cook for a further 10 minutes, stirring occasionally,
until the vegetables have softened.

mix

Add the rice, coconut milk, beans and sea salt,
and mix well. Bring to the boil, then cover and cook
for 40 minutes. Serve hot.

16

roti

makes ●●●●

prep

rest

cook

ingredients

250g (9oz/generous 1¾ cups)
  plain (all-purpose) flour
1 tsp baking powder
½ tsp sea salt
3 Tbsp vegetable oil

mix

Mix the flour, baking powder and salt together,
then add 140ml (5fl oz/scant ⅔ cup) water. Stir and
work with your hands to form a soft dough. Cover
and rest at room temperature for 30 minutes.

divide

Divide the dough into 8 pieces and, using your
hands, flatten each one into an 8-cm (3¼-in) circle.
Dip each circle into the oil on both sides, then
press them together gently to make a pair. Roll
each of the 4 pairs out until very thin and the size
of a small dinner plate.

fry

Heat a large heavy-based frying pan on a medium
heat, then one by one, fry the roti for 1–2 minutes
on each side until golden brown spots appear and
the surface stops looking translucent. Remove
and keep warm while you cook the remaining roti.

17

pikliz
(haiti)

serves

prep

marinate **x1**

ingredients
½ green cabbage, very finely
   sliced
1 red onion, very finely sliced
1 medium carrot, very finely
   sliced
2 red Scotch bonnet chillies,
   deseeded and very
   finely sliced
3 cloves garlic, minced
1 Tbsp black peppercorns
5 cloves
1 scant Tbsp sea salt
juice of 1 lime
200ml (7fl oz/scant 1 cup)
   white wine vinegar

marinate
Mix all the ingredients in a bowl, and leave to
marinate at room temperature for at least 1 hour
before eating. This will keep well for up to a week
in an airtight container in the fridge. Serve with
any of the jerk dishes in the book.

18

fried
bake

ingredients

300g (10½oz/2¼ cups) plain
  (all-purpose) flour
2 tsp baking powder
1 tsp sea salt
½ tsp caster (granulated) sugar
20g (¾oz/1½ Tbsp) cold
  butter, cubed

500ml (17fl oz/generous 2 cups)
  vegetable oil, to deep-fry

mix

Mix the flour, baking powder, salt and sugar
together. Add the butter and work together
with your hands until the mixture resembles
breadcrumbs. Gradually add 155ml (5fl oz/⅔ cup)
water and work together for 2 minutes until it is a
smooth dough.

rest

Place the dough in an oiled bowl, cover and leave
to rest at room temperature for 30 minutes.

fry

Heat the oil in a large wok to 180°C (350°F), or
until a cube of bread fizzes and turns a light golden
brown within 30 seconds. Divide the dough into
8 portions, and roll each into a flattened disc, about
8cm (3¼in) wide. Fry 2–3 pieces of dough at a
time for 30–40 seconds on each side until golden
brown. Drain on kitchen paper and continue with
the rest of the dough. Serve with curry.

jerk sweet potato fries

serves

prep

cook

ingredients

700g (1lb 9oz) sweet potato,
    peeled and cut into fries
2 Tbsp vegetable oil
1 Tbsp jerk seasoning
    (see page 115)
1 tsp sea salt

roast

Preheat the oven to 200°C (400°F). Mix the sweet potato fries, oil, jerk seasoning and salt together in a large roasting dish. Roast in the oven for about 35–45 minutes until crisp and golden brown.

serve

Serve hot with the Chicken Curry (see page 60) and Green Seasoning (see page 110).

(curries)

20

chicken curry
(jamaica)

ingredients

3 cloves garlic, minced

5cm (2in) ginger, minced

1 Scotch bonnet chilli, deseeded
  and minced

3 Tbsp Jamaican curry powder
  (see page 112)

juice of 1 lemon

600g (1lb 5oz) skinless,
  boneless chicken thighs, diced

2 Tbsp vegetable oil

1 onion, finely sliced

2 Tbsp tomato purée (paste)

400ml (14fl oz/1⅔ cups)
  coconut milk

350g (12oz) floury (mealy)
  potatoes, thinly sliced

2 tsp sea salt

marinate

Mix the garlic, ginger, chilli, curry powder and lemon juice together and scrape into a freezer bag. Add the chicken pieces and scrunch until the chicken is covered in the paste. Chill in the fridge for 1 hour, or overnight.

stir-fry

Heat the oil in a large saucepan, add the onion and stir-fry for 10 minutes on a medium heat until golden brown. Add the marinated chicken and stir-fry for a further 3–4 minutes to cook off the spices.

simmer

Stir through the tomato purée, then add the coconut milk, potatoes, 100ml (3½fl oz/7 Tbsp) water and salt. Bring to the boil, then reduce the heat to a low simmer, cover and cook for 30 minutes until the chicken and potatoes are cooked through. Serve with white rice or Rice and Peas (see page 39).

61 /

21

curry goat

serves

prep

marinate **x1**

cook **x3**

ingredients
500g (1lb 2oz) diced goat
  or mutton or lamb
4 Tbsp Jamaican curry powder
  (see page 112)
4 cloves garlic, minced
5cm (2in) ginger, minced
4 spring onions (scallions),
  finely chopped
3 Tbsp vegetable oil
1 onion, sliced
4–5 sprigs thyme
2 Tbsp tomato purée (paste)
400ml (14fl oz/1⅔ cups)
  beef stock
1 Scotch bonnet chilli, pierced
2 medium potatoes, peeled and
  cut into 5-cm (2-in) chunks
1–2 tsp sea salt

marinate
Mix the goat, curry powder, garlic, ginger and
spring onions together. Cover and chill for 1 hour,
or overnight.

brown
Preheat the oven to 150°C (300°F). Heat just
1 tablespoon of oil in a frying pan, add half the goat
and fry for 8–9 minutes, turning once to brown the
meat on both sides. Transfer to a lidded casserole
dish. Repeat with the remaining meat.

fry
Heat the remaining oil and fry the onion and thyme
for 10 minutes, stirring occasionally, before stirring
in the tomato purée. Transfer to the casserole, add
the stock and chilli and stir. Bring to the boil, then
cook in the oven for 2 hours. Add the potatoes,
and return to the oven for 1 hour. Taste and adjust
the salt. Serve with Rice and Peas (see page 39).

vegetable rundown

(jamaica)

serves ●●●●

prep

cook

ingredients

2 Tbsp vegetable oil
1 onion, finely sliced
4 spring onions (scallions),
  finely sliced
2 cloves garlic, finely chopped
1 Scotch bonnet chilli, deseeded
  and finely chopped
4 sprigs thyme
1 sweet potato, sliced into
  5-mm (¼-in) half moons
2 courgettes (zucchini), sliced
  into 1-cm (½-in) circles
2 ears sweetcorn, kernels only
400ml (14fl oz/1⅔ cups)
  coconut milk
2 tsp sea salt
freshly ground black pepper

heat

Heat the oil in a large saucepan, add the onion,
spring onions, garlic, chilli and thyme and stir well,
then cover and soften for 10 minutes, stirring
occasionally.

cook

Add the sweet potato, courgettes, sweetcorn,
coconut milk and salt and stir well. Cover and cook
for 20 minutes until the sweet potato is just tender.
Taste and season with salt and pepper as needed.
Serve with rice or Rice and Peas (see page 39).

note

You can use your preferred mix of vegetables in the
rundown – okra, carrots, peppers, etc.

23

oxtail curry

serves

prep

cook **x3**

ingredients

1kg (2lb 3oz) sliced oxtail
2 Tbsp vegetable oil
1 onion, roughly chopped
4 spring onions (scallions),
  roughly chopped
2 cloves garlic, finely chopped
4 sprigs thyme
2 Tbsp Jamaican curry powder
  (see page 112)
1 Scotch bonnet chilli, pierced
500ml (17fl oz/generous 2 cups)
  beef stock
1 Tbsp Worcestershire sauce
sea salt and freshly ground
  black pepper

brown

Preheat the oven to 150°C (300°F). Season the oxtail well with salt and pepper. Heat 1 tablespoon oil in a large frying pan and, working in batches, fry the oxtail for 3–4 minutes on each side until well browned, transferring the browned meat to a casserole dish as you go.

fry

In the same pan, heat another tablespoon oil, then add the onion, spring onions, garlic and thyme and stir-fry for 10 minutes until golden brown. Add the curry powder and stir-fry for 1 minute.

cook

Tip the onions into the casserole dish along with the chilli, and pour over the stock and Worcestershire sauce. Bring to the boil, then cover and cook in the oven for 3 hours. Taste and season with salt and black pepper. Serve with rice.

24

pumpkin curry

serves

prep

cook **x1**

ingredients

2 Tbsp vegetable oil
1 onion, finely sliced
5 cloves garlic, crushed
1kg (2lb 3oz) calabaza pumpkin
   or butternut squash, peeled,
   deseeded and cut into
   1.5-cm (½-in) chunks
1 Scotch bonnet chilli, deseeded
   and roughly chopped
1 tsp sea salt
1 tsp dark brown sugar
1 tsp ground cumin

pinch extra ground roasted
   cumin

soften

Heat the oil in a saucepan with a tight-fitting lid,
add the onion and garlic, cover and leave to soften
on a low–medium heat for 10 minutes, stirring
occasionally.

cook

Add the pumpkin, chilli, salt, sugar and cumin. Stir
well, cover and cook on a low heat for 40 minutes,
stirring once or twice until the pumpkin is soft.

mash

Mash the pumpkin with the back of a wooden
spoon, then cook, uncovered for a further
10 minutes until reduced, stirring occasionally.

season

Taste and season with salt as needed. Sprinkle
with the ground roasted cumin before serving.

25

brown stew fish

serves

prep

marinate **x1**

cook

ingredients

360g (12½oz) red snapper
   or sea bass fillets, skin on
1 onion, finely sliced
3 spring onions (scallions),
   finely sliced
3 cloves garlic, finely chopped
2.5cm (1in) ginger, finely
   chopped
3 sprigs thyme
1 large vine tomato, sliced
1 yellow (bell) pepper,
   finely sliced
juice of 1 lime
1 tsp freshly ground black
   pepper
1 tsp sea salt

2 Tbsp vegetable oil

mix

Place all the ingredients, except the oil, in a large bowl and gently mix to coat the fish in the vegetables. Cover and refrigerate for 1 hour. Remove the fish from the vegetables, reserving them for later.

fry

Heat 1 tablespoon of the oil in a large frying pan, add the fish and fry for 2 minutes on each side until just cooked through. Transfer to a plate.

cook

Add the remaining oil to the pan, then add the reserved vegetables and stir-fry for 5–6 minutes on a high heat. Add 100ml (3½fl oz/7 Tbsp) water, cover and cook for a further 5 minutes. Return the fish to the pan and cook with the vegetables for 2 minutes. Season and serve hot with white rice.

26

baigan choka

(indo-caribbean)

serves ●●

prep

cook

ingredients

1 aubergine (eggplant)
1 clove garlic, thinly sliced
1 Scotch bonnet chilli
1 Tbsp vegetable oil
½ white onion, finely chopped
1 tsp sea salt

roast

Preheat the oven to 220°C (425°F). Make a series of slits in the aubergine and stick the garlic slices in them. Transfer the aubergine to a roasting dish with the chilli and rub all over with the oil. Roast in the oven for 45 minutes, turning once.

crush

After 10 minutes, remove the chilli from the dish and carefully halve and remove the seeds. Crush in a mortar and pestle along with the sea salt, then set aside.

mash

Once the aubergine is blackened all over, remove from the oven and carefully cut in half. Scoop out the flesh into a bowl and mash with the back of a fork. Stir through the onions and chilli paste to taste, with more salt as needed. Serve hot with Roti (see page 50).

green
bean
curry

serves

prep

cook

ingredients
2 Tbsp vegetable oil
1 onion, finely sliced
2 cloves garlic, finely chopped
2.5cm (1in) ginger, finely
    chopped
½ Scotch bonnet chilli,
    deseeded and finely chopped
1 tsp Jamaican curry powder
    (see page 112)
300g (10½oz) green beans,
    trimmed
1 tsp sea salt

stir-fry
Heat the oil in a large saucepan, add the onion, garlic, ginger and chilli and stir-fry on a medium heat for 10 minutes until the onion is golden brown and softened.

simmer
Add the curry powder and stir-fry for a further minute, before adding the green beans and 100ml (3½fl oz/7 Tbsp) water. Stir briefly, then cover and cook for 6–7 minutes until the green beans are just cooked through. Uncover and simmer for a further minute to evaporate the remaining water. Season to taste with the salt, and serve hot with Rice and Peas (see page 39).

28

mackerel
rundown

serves

prep

cook

ingredients

400ml (14fl oz/1⅔ cups)
   coconut milk
1 onion, finely sliced
3 spring onions (scallions),
   finely sliced
1 Scotch bonnet chilli,
   deseeded and finely sliced
2 cloves garlic, minced
2 tomatoes, finely chopped
4 mackerel fillets
1 tsp sea salt

boil

Bring the coconut milk to the boil in a large saucepan
and boil on a medium heat for 20 minutes until
reduced by half – the milk will resemble custard
at this point.

cook

Add the onion, spring onions, chilli and garlic, then
partially cover and cook in the thickened coconut
milk for 5–6 minutes until softened. Add the
tomatoes and cook for a further minute before
adding the mackerel fillets and salt.

simmer

Reduce the heat, cover and cook on a low simmer
for 5–6 minutes until the mackerel is cooked
through. Taste and season with salt as needed,
and serve hot.

mackerel rundown

(big dishes)

jerk chicken

serves ●●●●●

prep ◔

marinate **x1**

cook **x1** ◑

ingredients
3 Tbsp jerk seasoning
  (see page 115)
2 tsp sea salt
2 Tbsp dark brown sugar
3 spring onions (scallions),
  roughly chopped
½ white onion, roughly chopped
3 cloves garlic, peeled
5cm (2in) ginger, peeled
1–2 Scotch bonnet chillies,
  deseeded
3 Tbsp vegetable oil
1kg (2lb 3oz) free-range chicken
  thighs and drumsticks

blitz
Blitz all the ingredients, except the chicken, in a food processor to a paste. Rub the paste all over the chicken, put the chicken in a bowl, cover and refrigerate for 1 hour, or overnight.

roast
Preheat the oven to 180°C (350°F). Transfer the marinated chicken to a roasting dish and roast in the oven for 1 hour. Increase the oven temperature to 200°C (400°F) and roast for a further 30 minutes to crisp the skin.

rest
Remove the chicken from the oven and leave to rest for a few minutes before serving hot with Pikliz (see page 51) or Rice and Peas (see page 39).

30

fire engine
(bahamas)

serves ●●●●

prep

cook

ingredients
2 Tbsp vegetable oil
500g (1lb 2oz) corned or minced
  (ground) beef
1 onion, finely chopped
1 stick celery, finely chopped
1 green (bell) pepper, finely
  chopped
50g (1¾oz) tomato purée (paste)
2 tsp sea salt
freshly ground black pepper

fry
Heat the oil in a large frying pan, add the beef
and fry on a medium heat for 10 minutes, breaking
up the meat with the back of a wooden spoon,
until well browned.

simmer
Add the onion, celery and pepper and stir-fry for a
further 10 minutes to soften. Add the tomato purée,
stir briefly, then add 500ml (17fl oz/generous 2
cups) water and simmer uncovered for 20 minutes.
Taste and season with more salt, and pepper as
needed, and serve with rice.

31

ackee & saltfish

serves ●●●●●

prep

soak **x4**

cook

ingredients

250g (9oz) salted cod
2 Tbsp vegetable oil
1 onion, finely sliced
3 spring onions (scallions),
  finely sliced
3 cloves garlic, finely chopped
2 sprigs thyme
1 red (bell) pepper, finely sliced
1 yellow (bell) pepper, finely
  sliced
1 Scotch bonnet chilli,
  deseeded and finely
  chopped
1 x 540-g (19-oz) can ackee,
  drained and gently rinsed
freshly ground black pepper

soak

Place the salted cod in a bowl of cold water, and soak for 4 hours, changing the water every hour.

fry

Heat the oil in a large frying pan, add the onion, spring onions, garlic, thyme, peppers and chilli and stir-fry for 10–12 minutes on a medium heat until softened.

shred

Pulse the drained saltfish in a food processor to shred, then add to the peppers together with the ackee. Stir-fry for a further 5 minutes, then taste and season with black pepper. Serve with Fried Bake (see page 54) and Plantain Wedges (see page 46).

32

bbq ribs

serves

prep

marinate **x6**

cook **x1**

ingredients
2 x 500-g (1lb 2-oz) rack of ribs

½ onion, roughly chopped
4 spring onions (scallions),
  roughly chopped
4 cloves garlic, peeled
5cm (2in) ginger, peeled
2 Scotch bonnet chillies,
  deseeded
3 Tbsp dark brown sugar
1 Tbsp Dijon mustard
3 Tbsp tomato purée (paste)
2 Tbsp Worcestershire sauce
2 Tbsp white wine vinegar
1 Tbsp dried thyme
1 tsp grated nutmeg
1 Tbsp ground allspice
2 tsp sea salt
good grind black pepper

blitz
Tip all the ingredients, except the ribs, into a food
processor and blitz until it is a thick sauce. Rub
the barbecue sauce all over the ribs, put in a bowl,
cover and refrigerate for 6 hours, or overnight.

roast
When ready to cook, preheat the oven to 170°C
(325°F). Place the ribs in a roasting dish, cover
tightly with foil and roast for 1 hour 30 minutes.

barbecue
To finish the ribs, either transfer to a barbecue and
cook until well charred on both sides or uncover
and increase the oven temperature to 200°C
(400°F) for a further 20 minutes until well browned.

serve
Slice the ribs and serve immediately with Pikliz
(see page 51) or Rice and Peas (see page 39).

87

33

ropa vieja

(cuba)

serves

prep

cook **x2**

ingredients
2 Tbsp vegetable oil
600g (1lb 5oz) flank or bavette
  steaks
1 onion, finely chopped
3 cloves garlic, finely chopped
2 sticks celery, finely chopped
1 carrot, finely chopped
1 green (bell) pepper, finely
  sliced
1 Tbsp tomato purée (paste)
1 x 400-g (14-oz) can chopped
  tomatoes
500ml (17fl oz/generous 2 cups)
  beef stock
290g (10oz/2⅓ cups) pimento-
  stuffed olives
sea salt and freshly ground
  black pepper

sear
Preheat the oven to 150°C (300°F). Heat half the oil in a large frying pan, add the steaks and sear well on each side for 3–4 minutes. Transfer to a casserole dish.

stir-fry
Heat the remaining oil, then add the onion, garlic, celery and carrot and stir-fry on a medium heat for 10 minutes until golden brown. Add the green pepper and stir-fry for a further 3–4 minutes until softened. Stir in the tomato purée and cook for a further minute, before tipping into the casserole dish with the steak.

bake
Add the chopped tomatoes and stock and stir well. Cook in the oven for 2 hours, adding the olives for the final 30 minutes. Shred the meat with 2 forks, and season to taste. Serve with white rice.

91

34

albondigon
(puerto rico)

serves

prep

cook

ingredients

3 eggs
1 Tbsp olive oil
2 cloves garlic, finely sliced
1 x 400-g (14-oz) can chopped
   tomatoes
1 tsp sea salt

2 eggs
500g (1lb 2oz) minced (ground)
   beef
1 onion, finely chopped
4 cloves garlic, finely chopped
50g (1¾oz/scant 1 cup) fresh
   white breadcrumbs, soaked
   in 100ml (3½fl oz/7 Tbsp) milk
1 Tbsp English mustard
30g (1oz/½ cup) fresh parsley,
   finely chopped
2 tsp sea salt
1 Tbsp freshly ground black
   pepper

boil

Boil 3 of the eggs for 8 minutes, before placing in a bowl of cold water and peeling when cool enough to handle.

fry

Meanwhile, heat the oil in a saucepan, add the garlic and fry for a few seconds before adding the tomatoes and salt. Simmer on a high heat for 30 minutes until well reduced.

beat

For the meatloaf, preheat the oven to 180°C (350°F). Line a 900-g (2-lb) loaf pan with greaseproof paper. Beat the remaining 2 eggs and mix with the beef, onion, garlic, breadcrumbs, mustard, parsley, salt and pepper. To check the seasoning, fry 1 teaspoon of the mixture and taste it – add more salt and pepper as needed.

press

Press half of the mixture down into the loaf pan, and make 3 indentations for the eggs in the middle. Place the eggs in the indentations, then gently press the remaining meat around the eggs. Cook in the oven for 25 minutes.

cook

After 25 minutes, spread the reduced tomato sauce over the meatloaf, then return to the oven to cook for a further 10 minutes. Remove the meatloaf from the pan and serve hot or cold.

35

oil down
with chicken

(grenada)

serves

prep

cook

ingredients

1kg (2lb 3oz) skinless, boneless
   chicken thighs, diced
70g (2½oz) bacon lardons
1 onion, roughly sliced
1 stick celery, roughly chopped
3 cloves garlic, finely chopped
2 carrots, sliced
1 Scotch bonnet chilli,
   deseeded and finely chopped
4 sprigs thyme
½ tsp ground turmeric
1 x 540-g (19-oz) can sliced
   breadfruit, drained and rinsed
2 tsp sea salt
800ml (27fl oz/3⅓ cups)
   coconut milk
100g (3½oz) spinach, roughly
   chopped

assemble

Layer the chicken, bacon, onion, celery, garlic,
carrots, chilli, thyme, turmeric, breadfruit chunks
and salt in a large lidded saucepan. Pour over
the coconut milk, and bring to the boil.

simmer

Reduce the heat to a low simmer, partially cover
with the lid and cook for 30 minutes. Throw over
the spinach, then cook, uncovered, for a further
5 minutes. Serve hot with rice or Festival Fried
Dumplings (see page 26).

note

Traditionally, salt pork is used in oil down, but as
this is not readily available, this recipe substitutes
bacon lardons.

36

goat water
(montserrat)

serves

prep

cook **x2**

ingredients
1 Tbsp vegetable oil
500g (1lb 2oz) diced goat
  or mutton
1 onion, finely chopped
2 sticks celery, finely chopped
3 cloves garlic, finely chopped
2 Tbsp plain (all-purpose) flour
2 Tbsp tomato purée (paste)
750ml (25fl oz/3 cups)
  beef stock
2 Scotch bonnet chillies, pierced
sea salt and freshly ground
  black pepper

brown
Preheat the oven to 150°C (300°F). Heat the oil in a large frying pan and, working in 2 batches, brown the meat on a medium heat for 3–4 minutes on each side before transferring to a casserole dish.

stir-fry
Add the onion, celery and garlic to the frying pan, and stir-fry on a medium heat for 10 minutes until golden brown. Add the flour and tomato purée and stir-fry for a further 2 minutes.

tip
Tip the onion mixture into the casserole dish with the goat, add the stock and chillies, stir well and season with salt and pepper. Bring to the boil, then cover and cook in the oven for 2 hours. Remove the chillies before serving with Festival Fried Dumplings (see page 26) or white rice.

37

jerk pulled pork

serves ●●●
●●●
●●●

prep

marinate x6

cook x6

ingredients
1.2kg (2lb 12oz) shoulder of pork

3 Tbsp dark brown sugar
6 cloves garlic, peeled
10 sprigs thyme, leaves only
4 spring onions (scallions)
2 Scotch bonnet chillies,
   deseeded
3 Tbsp jerk seasoning
   (see page 115)
50ml (1¾fl oz/scant ¼ cup)
   dark rum
1 Tbsp sea salt

blitz
Blitz the sugar, garlic, thyme, onions, chillies, jerk seasoning, rum and salt in a food processor, or finely mince the larger ingredients and mix in a bowl to make the jerk marinade.

rub
Rub the marinade all over the pork, then cover and refrigerate for 6 hours, or overnight.

cook
When ready to cook, preheat the oven to 140°C (250°F). Transfer the pork to a lidded casserole dish, cover and cook for 6 hours until tender.

rest
Remove the pork from the oven and leave to rest for 15 minutes, before transferring to a board, and using 2 forks to shred the meat.

jerk pulled pork

38 boliche

(cuba)

makes

prep

marinate **x2**

cook **x3**

ingredients

1.6kg (3lb 8oz) silverside
or topside joint
8 cloves garlic
2 Tbsp oregano leaves
(2 tsp dried)
2 tsp sea salt
2 Tbsp olive oil
1 Tbsp orange juice
1 Tbsp lime juice
1 Tbsp freshly ground black
pepper
160g (5¾oz) chorizo,
roughly chopped
200ml (7fl oz/scant 1 cup)
white wine
2 onions, roughly sliced
2 bay leaves
600ml (20fl oz/2½ cups)
beef stock
750g (1lb 10oz) new potatoes

marinate

Turn the joint over, and make a long cut as deep
as the centre of the meat, so it opens out flat like
a book. Mash the garlic, oregano and salt with a
pestle and mortar, then mix with the oil, orange
juice, lime juice and pepper. Rub the marinade
well into the meat, then put in a bowl, cover and
refrigerate for 2 hours, or ideally overnight.

roll

When ready to cook, preheat the oven to 150°C
(300°F). Place the chopped chorizo in the middle
of the joint, roll the meat tightly around it and
secure with kitchen string.

cook

Heat a large casserole dish, large enough to
comfortably hold the beef, and sear the joint on
a high heat for 2–3 minutes on each side until
evenly browned. Pour the wine into the pan and
let it bubble down for 2 minutes, before adding
the onions, bay leaves, stock and new potatoes.
Bring to the boil, then cover and cook in the oven
for 3 hours, turning the joint over halfway through
cooking. Serve the meat sliced with the gravy
and potatoes alongside.

39

escovitch fish

(jamaica)

makes

prep

cook

ingredients

2 sea bream or red snapper
juice of 1 lime
sea salt and freshly ground
  black pepper

3 Tbsp vegetable oil
1 onion, finely sliced
1 red (bell) pepper, cut into
  fine strips
1 green (bell) pepper, cut into
  fine strips
1 carrot, cut into fine strips
1 Scotch bonnet chilli,
  deseeded and thinly sliced
1 tsp allspice berries
100ml (3½fl oz/7 Tbsp) malt
  vinegar
1 tsp sea salt

rub

Cut 2 slashes on each side of the red snapper,
then rub with the lime juice, salt and pepper.
Refrigerate while you prepare the vegetables.

fry

Heat the oil in a large frying pan on a medium heat,
add the fish and fry for 5 minutes on each side.
transfer to a plate and keep warm in a low oven.

stir-fry

Add the onion, peppers, carrot and chilli to the
frying pan and stir-fry on a high heat for about
5–6 minutes until the vegetables are just turning
soft. Add the allspice berries, vinegar and salt and
simmer for 2–3 minutes.

serve

Tip the vegetables and liquid over the fish, and
serve immediately.

(extras)

40

green seasoning

(trinidad & tobago)

serves

prep

ingredients

5 spring onions (scallions),
   roughly chopped
30g (1oz/½ cup) coriander
   (cilantro), leaves and stems
15g (½oz) bunch thyme,
   leaves only
4 cloves garlic, peeled
1 green (bell) pepper, roughly
   chopped
1 stick celery, roughly chopped
1 green Scotch bonnet chilli,
   deseeded
1 tsp sea salt
2 Tbsp vegetable oil

blitz

Place all the ingredients in a food processor with
2 tablespoons water and blitz until smooth.

serve

Taste and adjust the salt as needed, and serve
the sauce with any Caribbean dish. It is particularly
good alongside the Jerk Sweet Potato Fries
(see page 56) or any jerk dish. Store in the fridge
for up to a week.

jamaican curry powder

jars **x1**

prep

cook

ingredients

2 Tbsp ground turmeric
4 Tbsp coriander seeds
2 Tbsp cumin seeds
2 Tbsp yellow mustard seeds
1 Tbsp black peppercorns
1 Tbsp allspice berries
1 Tbsp fenugreek seeds
2 star anise

toast

Tip all the ingredients into a large frying pan and toast on a low–medium heat for 10 minutes, stirring every 2 minutes to ensure that all the spices toast evenly. Make sure they don't burn.

cool

Once lightly coloured and aromatic, transfer the spices to a plate to cool completely.

blitz

Once cool, blitz the spices in a spice grinder or with a pestle and mortar until finely ground. Store in an airtight jar for up to 2 months.

jerk seasoning

jars **x2**

prep

cook

ingredients

4 Tbsp dried thyme
2 Tbsp allspice berries
4 Tbsp black peppercorns
2 large cinnamon sticks
2 tsp cayenne pepper
2 tsp sea salt
½ nutmeg, freshly grated

fry

Place all ingredients in a large frying pan and heat on a medium heat for 7–8 minutes, stirring frequently until aromatic.

grind

Allow to cool, then grind in a spice grinder or with a pestle and mortar. Store in an airtight jar for up to 2 months.

43

pique
(puerto rico)

jars x1

prep

ingredients
300ml (10fl oz/1¼ cups)
   cider vinegar
½ tsp sea salt
5 Scotch bonnet chilies,
   pierced
5 jalapeño chillies, pierced
5 cloves garlic, peeled
1 tsp black peppercorns
1 bay leaf

mix
Mix the vinegar and sea salt together. Place
the chillies, garlic, peppercorns and bay leaf into
a 500-ml (17-fl oz) screw-top or clip-top jar, then
pour the vinegar over the top of all the ingredients.

marinate
Cover the jar, then leave to marinate for 3–4 days
before using the vinegar as a spicy condiment.
Once opened, store in the fridge for up to 2 weeks.

44

cuban mojo

serves

serves

prep

cook

ingredients

1 head garlic, peeled
1 tsp sea salt
1 tsp ground cumin
1 tsp dried oregano
1 tsp freshly ground black
 pepper
15ml (½fl oz/1 Tbsp)
 orange juice
15ml (½fl oz/1 Tbsp) lime juice
25ml (1fl oz/5 tsp) olive oil

mash

Mash the peeled garlic cloves with the salt, cumin, oregano and pepper using a pestle and mortar.

stir

Scrape the mixture into a bowl, and stir through the orange and lime juice.

fry

Heat the oil in a small pan until just warm, then stir this into the garlic mixture. Taste and add more salt and pepper as needed, and allow to cool to room temperature before storing in the fridge. This will keep for a week, and can be used as a marinade or sauce for meat and vegetables.

rum
punch
(jamaica)

serves

prep

ingredients
250ml (8½fl oz/1 cup) dark rum
250ml (8½fl oz/1 cup) white or
    coconut rum
130ml (4½fl oz/½ cup) grenadine
250ml (8½fl oz/1 cup) pineapple
    juice
200ml (7fl oz/scant 1 cup)
    orange juice
100ml (3½fl oz/7 Tbsp) lime juice
4–5 drops angostura bitters

orange/pineapple slices, to serve

mix
Mix all the ingredients together in a large jug,
and refrigerate until needed.

serve
Serve over ice with the orange/pineapple slices.

note
Double the quantities for more guests.

46

cuba libre

serves

prep

ingredients

handful ice cubes
1 lime
100ml (3½fl oz/7 Tbsp) rum
250ml (8½fl oz/1 cup) cola

muddle

Tip the ice cubes into 2 glasses, and squeeze the lime juice into them. Throw a squeezed lime half into each and muddle briefly with the end of a rolling pin to release the oil from the rind.

serve

Pour half the rum into each glass, followed by half the cola, stir briefly then serve.

(desserts)

47

coconut gizzada

serves

prep

cook

ingredients

200g (7oz) plain (all-purpose) flour
100g (3½oz/7 Tbsp) cold unsalted butter
½ tsp sea salt

100g (3½oz/scant 1½ cups) fresh grated coconut (or use desiccated/dry unsweetened coconut, rehydrated in water for 15 minutes and drained)
100g (3½oz/½ cup) dark brown sugar
½ tsp grated nutmeg
1 Tbsp unsalted butter

blitz

Blitz the flour, butter and salt in a food processor or work together with your hands until the mixture resembles fine sand. Add 2–3 tablespoons cold water, bit by bit, and mix until the pastry comes together. Cover and refrigerate for 20 minutes.

cook

Tip the coconut, sugar, nutmeg and 100ml (3½fl oz/7 Tbsp) water into a saucepan and bring to the boil. Stir occasionally for the next 10 minutes, then add the butter and cook for 5–6 minutes until thickened. Remove from the heat and set aside.

continued on the next page…

roll

Preheat the oven to 180°C (350°F) and butter a
12-hole muffin pan. Roll out the chilled pastry on a
lightly floured work surface until it is very thin, and
stamp out 8-cm (3¼-in) circles, transferring each
circle into the muffin pan. Repeat until all the pastry
is used up. Transfer to the oven to blind bake for
10 minutes.

bake

Fill each pastry case with a heaped tablespoon
of the coconut mixture, then return to the oven
to bake for a further 20 minutes. While still hot,
remove from the muffin pan to a wire rack to cool.

coconut toto

serves

prep

cook

ingredients

100g (3½oz/½ cup) dark
   brown sugar
100g (3½oz/7 Tbsp) unsalted
   butter, softened
1 tsp vanilla bean paste or
   extract
2 eggs
150ml (5fl oz/⅔ cup) milk
1 Tbsp dark rum
200g (7oz/1½ cups) plain
   (all-purpose) flour
100g (3½oz/1⅓ cups)
   desiccated (dry unsweetened)
   coconut
2 tsp baking powder
1 tsp ground ginger
½ tsp ground allspice
½ tsp ground nutmeg
½ tsp sea salt

beat

Preheat the oven to 180°C (350°F). Butter and
base line a 21 x 21-cm (8¼ x 8¼-in) square cake
pan. Beat the sugar, butter and vanilla bean paste
together in a large bowl until thoroughly mixed.
Beat in the eggs, one at a time, followed by the
milk and rum.

mix

Mix the flour, coconut, baking powder, spices and
salt together in another bowl. Tip into the sugar and
egg mixture and gently fold together to combine.

bake

Spoon the batter into the pan, then bake in the
oven for 30 minutes until golden brown. It is
cooked through when a cocktail stick is inserted
into the middle and comes out clean. Transfer to
a wire rack to cool, before cutting into 16 squares
and serving.

chow

serves

prep

marinate

ingredients

1 mango, not too ripe
½ clove garlic, finely minced
15g (½oz/¼ cup) coriander
  (cilantro) sprigs, finely chopped
1 Tbsp Trinidadian hot pepper
  sauce
juice of 1 lime
½ tsp sea salt
freshly ground black pepper

mix

Mix all the ingredients together in a bowl.

marinate

Transfer to the fridge to marinate for 30 minutes–
1 hour, then taste and adjust the levels of salt
and lime juice as required before serving at room
temperature.

50

arroz con dulce

serves ●●●●

prep ◑

soak **x2**

cook ◑

ingredients

200g (7oz/generous 1 cup)
  long-grain white rice
400ml (13½fl oz/1⅔ cups)
  evaporated milk
400ml (13½fl oz/1⅔ cups)
  coconut milk
75g (2¾oz/6 Tbsp) caster
  (granulated) sugar
6 cloves
1 stick cinnamon
1 tsp freshly grated nutmeg
1 tsp ground ginger

soak

Soak the rice in 3 times its volume of water for
2 hours, then drain well. Transfer to a saucepan
and cover in 3 times its volume of water again,
and bring to the boil. Reduce the heat and simmer
for 10 minutes, then drain well.

simmer

Tip the cooked rice back into the saucepan along
with the evaporated milk, coconut milk, sugar,
cloves, cinnamon, nutmeg and ginger. Bring to
the boil, then reduce the heat and simmer for
20 minutes, stirring constantly until thickened.
Taste and add a further few tablespoons of sugar
if you wish.

cool

Allow to cool, and serve at room temperature.

JERK BBQ CHICKEN WRAP

JERK BBQ CHICKEN SALAD

JERK VEGGIE BEAN CAKE WRAP

JERK VEGGIE BEAN CAKE SALAD

6 JERK BBQ CHICKEN WINGS

FRIED PLANTAIN